Tasin SCiva

Just 2 Assumptions

I, Volume 1

Tasin SCiva

Published by Tasin SCiva, 2024.

While every precaution has been taken in the preparation of this book, the publisher assumes no responsibility for errors or omissions, or for damages resulting from the use of the information contained herein.

JUST 2 ASSUMPTIONS

First edition. July 30, 2024.

ISBN: 979-8227320957

Written by Tasin SCiva.

Dedicated first to the ideal of goodness.

"Just 2 Assumptions"

Including the mass uprising of 2024

For The Wanderers (Suiciders)

Dedicated to those readers who will fully use this book to their own advantage

Look, if you really need or want the book, have money to buy the book and the ability to use that money to buy this book, buy it. It is the minimum price I could sell at. If you don't have any one of the latter two, just send me an email at tasinsciva346@gmail.com. If I am active, I will send you the book's pdf document for you, which you can share with others. Why would I do that? *"For all and for one"*. That's all the reason I need.

A Poem by Tasin SCiva

"The Wanderers of Life"

"Some of us keep wandering
On the streets of life, seeking
We do not know what it is
Perhaps only an angel's kiss
Or an angel's tear
Something we cannot bear.
Why do we meaninglessly vie?
When we all shall eventually die?
Some of us choose death
For it may be the better wraith.
But the truth is,
We only need a kiss.
A kiss by The Truth
To reignite the root.
Let seeking that be one of the reasons
To keep enduring life's seasons
Let that be our 'why',
So that we no longer cry.

And maybe, one day, we'll hopefully die,
Never again to vie.
Maybe, one day, we'll cry
That this was our 'why'.
And if anyone asks, "Who are you thus?"
Say to them, "The Wanderers of life are us."

My Starting Note to The Reader

Peace be upon you, my reader. Let the peace enter your chaotic interior and heal your messy exterior. Who am I? My pen name is ***Tasin SCiva***, the name you will know me by. Why am I here? ***"For the sake of goodness"*** - a reason you may not understand yet, but you will later, hopefully. How am I here? Same as you, perhaps slightly a bit better off than you are. What am I? A person, a writer, a dreamer, a philosopher and hopefully a true advisor to you.

But enough about me, let's talk about you. Who are you? Why are you here? How are you? What are you?

Answer that honestly to yourself, if not to me. Your intelligence, your potential and your ability are quite good.

How do I know that? Because you are like me, and I am like you. I too am a wanderer, or at least I was. By the time this book is out in the world, I hope that I am more than a wanderer and by the time you have read this book, I hope that you too will be more than a wanderer. I know you are like me, suicidal and randomly wandering on the roads inside us and outside us. If not, you are free to leave. If yes, then hold on just for a moment longer.

I know what you are thinking deep inside. ***Everything is nothing and nothing is everything.*** What's the point of living, striving and excelling? Why? Why and why and just why? That's all you can think about.

Let's fix that. No, let's answer that endless stream of questions and doubts, with an endless stream of answers and certainties. Others can't understand us yet, until they become like us. Who are we? Why are we here? Why, why and just why? The lack of force within makes everything be nothing to us. I know it, I feel it, and I sense it. That emptiness will not go away unless you can hold on to 2 simple assumptions, and always with them just 2 ideals. That's all my message is about. Just 2 assumptions. All you need to remind yourself every time you are lost and wandering are these 2 assumptions, nothing less and nothing more.

I know the cynic in you that doubts everything, even yourself, especially yourself. It doubts your perception, your own intelligence, your potential, your ability, your authorities, and everything including me and this book and this message.

I want to tell your cynic that it is absolutely and truly is right to question everything, to doubt everything, even the most basic knowledge we may have. Why? Because doubts are harmless if you believe and know the Truth to be absolute and true, and useful to root out falsehood. All you really need is a tiny bit of hope, a tiny bit of faith. But not blind faith nor illogical faith. In order to have truth faith, you need both your mind (logic) and your heart (inner feeling) to work. That's all I am here for. For you and for me—for the likes of us who go insane from our own intelligence, life and conscience. I am here to give you that tiniest bit of assurance that you are not the unique one with the unique mental instability, that you are part of a group of people (the Wanderers) and you'll soon be a part of a new group of people (the Seekers) . Don't worry, you don't have to talk to them, just know that they are like you. So, they'll accept you, however you are, wherever you are, whatever you are, for they too are travelers in the path of life and to the same destination of death and hopefully they will help, inspire and guide you to the Truth. Plus, it's all about them, about what you want, why you want it, how you want it and such. You want the end (Death), right? Good, I can provide you 1 thing, if nothing else, the only truth I can say to you without any deception or filters, is that you will absolutely

and truly get that death you are seeking. For now, just calm down and take a glimpse, just a glimpse of what truly is.........
. . . .
. . . .

Do you understand or know the above sign? No? Good. I'll teach you what it means and how it can save your life and most importantly, save you. I never really told you who I am. I only told you a name but that's just a name. If you really want to know who I am, find out for yourself from all the words you read. This is no guide to life, and I am indeed no expert, but I do have over 20 years of life experience, if that even means anything. And just during that time, I found out about everything and considered everything. How, you may ask? Well, come with me, I'll show you on the way.

Tasin SCiva

29th July 2024.

Contents

Chapter-0 (The Absolute)

The world, the life, the mind, the heart——everything -even 'nothing' is messy and chaotic. All of them are vulnerable to change, even you yourself, your knowledge, your most basic assumptions, perception, understanding etc.

What is truly the Absolute? The Eternal? The True? Everything we learn, even the words used here are just indicators to the real things. Like by the word 'tree' you understand a tree, that they are green and in forests and gardens and such. You get that idea in your mind. That's all language really is, just an indicator.

Words may not be able to express everything I may wish to express here to let you realize the Truth, but I'll try my best. In childhood, you held on to goodness, almost naturally, I guarantee you that. There are some things I know for sure, with absoluteness. So, I tell you that you were indeed a good and fulfilled person as a mere child.

But the world corrupted you and you, being naïve, let it corrupt you. The world tried to fill your mind with its own ideas and all. Now, all you say, think and are just a mirror of the world and its people.

Now you may think, 'Well, you are corrupting me with your idea'. **No, I am trying to inspire you.** How can you tell the difference?

Through the intentions of the people who try to instill something in you. What are their deepest intentions? I told you mine, "For all and for one". Why is that my intention, you may ask?

Well, otherwise I couldn't live solely for myself. I myself am not that worthy, living for and striving for. So, I live for others and myself. They add value to my existence, just enough so that I do not get lost in darkness ever again. I would recommend you try it, but later.

Now, let's go back to the message. But if you still doubt me, I'll give you a little example to calm your cynical mind down. Will you trust the man who is trying to get your attention for solely himself (like for his own profits, interests and such) so that he can hammer his ideas into your mind or will you trust the man who simply is letting a concept sit right in front of you and lets you choose for yourself, try it out and even leave it if doesn't fit you?

Just for clarity, I am the latter one. Out of seemingly endless books of seemingly endless time, I am only presenting you a concept, that I believe, can help you, even if just a little bit. So, if you can use it, please use it. But if you won't, I only request 2 things from you, nothing else. Just 2 things, hold on tightly to the Truth and to your life, and I promise you will be saved from something you will greatly regret and greatly fear.

How do I know that? Like I said, I know some things with absoluteness. That's why I said it. And if you hate the message, it's fine. You can burn the message or even preach to others that it is the worst book ever and no one should read it. I am fine by all of that, because truth be told, I personally don't care, as long as those who need the message get the message.

Now, we got quite a bit distracted from the main topic here. So, as I was saying, you are basically an echo of the world and the people in it. I tell you first to forsake all of that, basically get out of their realm of influences within you, even the influence of yourself, and imagine yourself standing right outside a house, the house which is all of your influences and such. Now to find out the Absolute, we need to focus a bit.

Blind, mindless faith is not absolute , nor right. We each have a thirst for more, both emotionally and intellectually. You must realize that everything changes, nothing stays permanently as it is. It all changes, even the most reliable scientific knowledge, so it is safe to assume that all of it will change. (Newton was considered the most reliable authority in Physics until Einstein came along and proved Newton wrong. Currently, Einstein is the most reliable authority, and we can safely assume that even that may change.)

Let's base all of it on 'change'. Next, something or someone may be absolute at it. So, is the 'change' absolute? It is a good choice, but let's assume that the 'Absolute' itself is the Absolute. After all, something must be absolute, even if that absolute is 'nothingness', it is absolute empty space. So, by broadening the definition of 'Absolute', we can finally stand on something absolute. Let the 1st assumption be "The Absolute is truly the Absolute, undoubtedly." – just a statement but internalize it to your mind and heart. It should calm you down from within- a sure statement which is multidimensional but still correct to its core.

Of course, the absolute is the absolute, it is obvious! It is obvious but remember when I told you that we question even our knowledge and perceptions and everything. This is all to give you an absolute reference point which will not change, at least not in concept. Now, let's move on, "The Absolute is truly the Absolute, undoubtedly," – the surety, certainty, the logic , the inner feeling you get from internalizing this statement , I now want you to project it to everything else. At least from that absolute point, you are sure of your new point's position—it's not absolute, just a referenced point, under the domain of the Absolute.

Now what is truly the Absolute, the Eternal, the True? The name may change, the language may change, even we may change, even all can change, but the concept, the idea the theory itself will remain unchanged absolutely , permanently, and truly for all cases without exception.

So, what did we achieve here? A sense of certainty, surety and absoluteness through mere language.

If you have not achieved it, then go back and reread the above statements carefully again. You are intelligent, understanding and learned. And if you cannot do it, let your inner cynic arise to help you. You can do it if you truly try, hopefully.

Many say that God is the Absolute, some say science is the Absolute, But I tell you now, that only the Absolute itself is the Absolute, undoubtedly. It is first of all, a concept in your mind and inner self, an absolute theory you cannot question nor doubt as it is utterly obvious like saying "x = x".

No matter what angle you look at it from, it is logical, simple and obvious. But even then, in case you are like me, who questions even this statement, I tell you to take it as an assumption, an idea, a theory that basically says "x = x" in math.

Chapter-1 (DEATH)

Death is the only absolute truth of life.

The sense of certainty, surety and absoluteness, you got from the previous chapter, apply it here at the above statement. Really focus and internalize the statement. Indeed, death is the absolute truth of life. Moreover, it can come at anytime, anywhere and anyhow. Yet you will see us so busy with our lives that we even forget death is there.

I know you may be getting bored. So to help you focus, I'll tell you a story. Do you want a true story or a fictional one? Normally, I myself prefer the latter one. It helps me escape the reality of life and death. But here, I'll tell you a true story, from my own life experience.

Let me warn you from the start, my life has been mostly boring, because truth be told, I hate surprises, not the pleasant ones, just the unpleasant ones.

In childhood, I was pretty open, kind and generous even. I was basically naïve. Whatever came, I simply endured it and went through life without really internalizing anything. I was smart, I was a topper.

But that was only because my parents and teachers really forced me to use my talents for learning and studying. And without thinking much, I simply obeyed them in every sphere of life. I realize now that I trusted them to know what was best for me. But later when the Covid pandemic hit the world, all of my trust, my certainty and my naiveness was destroyed in a span of long, hard and painful months. I could not trust anyone anymore, especially not myself who trusted them in the first place. I had major exams coming up before the Covid pandemic hit and I was supposed to be one of the best students at the best college in my country, to prepare like a topper and ace the exams.

But when the exams were cancelled dend delayed, and people I knew started dying around me. It made me uneasy, anxious and doubtful inside. So much so that I could not focus on studies any longer, I instead chose ways of numbing all these anxieties within, with something and really anything.

Whether it was games, or movies or series and any number of stuffs on the internet, I became obsessed with things and lived entirely in a different reality. One that was uncertain and I the most unstable factor in it. Although others who saw me, saw a young boy drowning himself in debauchery, I saw myself as a young boy trying to get as far as possible from my reality. They saw me enjoying all the good stuff of life, easily breezing through life and expecting great results in my online exams. But only I knew what I was then, I became a pretender, a liar, a cheater and the worst self I could ever be. I never want to be that self ever again.

Later my father, the only breadwinner of my family, became infected with Coronavirus. But that was to be expected, he is a doctor, who saw the ills of Coronavirus firsthand everyday they went to the hospital. But I was not exactly sad or devastated that my father was ill, most likely to die at any time then. I didn't go to his room, didn't serve him nor care for him during that critical time of his life when he could have died anytime. I actually felt nothing in me, no emotion at all even though both logically and emotionally it was a critical time. Logically speaking, if he had died then like so many died every day , my family was doomed. None of us had any jobs nor any property where we could safely take shelter at. Not just that, emotionally I should have felt something, if not for the material stuff, at least for the fact that he was my father, who was always kind to me and my role model. I should have felt sad at the very least, but truth be told, I felt nothing. Nothing for the fact he could most likely die at any time then. Nothing for the fact that my family would fall to financial ruin then. Nothing for the fact that I would have to quit my studies and start working then. Nothing at all. Why? Now that I look back on it, I now know why. I was too disconnected to my reality to actually process it and moreover, I was successfully numbed from the inside out due to all my addictions.

I had no humanity left in me, no fellow feeling, no empathy, no care at all for anything or anyone even myself. My mother was too busy caring for my father to notice. So I used to get out some days and wander the empty , desolate streets by myself, perhaps internally wishing for something, anything or someone , anyone, to just somehow bring me the thing I lost. I once even moved directly towards a large bus on the opposite lane. As the bus was moving right towards me at high speed, I increased my own speed and rushed to it directly facing its front side on the main road. I still cannot tell why I suddenly did it. It made no sense, because I looked fine. In fact, I was in a vacation with my family, so why would I suddenly go away from my family and do this dangerous thing?

The same reason why I moved away at the last moment. I couldn't do it. I still wanted to figure out why and how it happened. I could not kill myself until I found out and defined exactly why I want to choose this path over life.

So I lived. I endured and I endured life and helplessness within. It's not like I didn't have friends, in fact, I had many friends. But the problem is, I couldn't talk to them about this. Why? Simple, they would laugh at me and say I am being too dramatic or too pragmatic. I know how they are; they are too far from where I was.

Plus, truth be told, I didn't consider any of them my true friends. After all, friends are those who stick their necks out for each other, do each other favors for no reason at all. But they only used to use me. How do I know that?

Well, when you are a topper or a rich person or great enough, it's obvious why you get so many friends all of a sudden. I don't classify those who are just there to take advantage of me as my friends, I call them 'acquaintances'. Nor do I classify those partners as my lovers who are also just there to take advantage of me , they are just 'addictive substances' to me, no more no less.

So, you understand why I like to stay as far as possible from both. The world is not all bubbles and glitters. It only seemed that way when we were little. Now we see for the world for what it truly is, a devils' lair. Almost everywhere you will find selfish people doing selfish things. Selflessness is an ideal we lost long ago. If you think like that, nowadays people call you 'foolhardy'. No, they are the fools who live for selfish reasons and die for selfish reasons. They are the fools who have no beautiful ideal to hold on to. Let them mock me, let them mock us , who are disillusioned with this world and its selfish people. We will show them soon enough, who's really right and who's really wrong. So endure, but do not submit like I once did. Always stand for the beautiful ideals, stand for goodness and believe in it. I promise you on my ideals, you will not regret being good, but you will regret being wrong, for I have my life experience to prove it.

Now back to my story, I wanted to figure out the big questions, stuff which I could not name by language. But I had no idea how to do that. So, what happened? Well, the pandemic ended and so I returned to my normal life, struggling to make up for the lost time and focus. But I went on to again achieve an excellent result in my examination, and yet, I felt no joy inside like how I used to feel before. I still felt nothing but I avoided confronting it and again indulged in debauchery. But this time, I still went out to figure out some things.

But later, it was proved that it was not enough. How? Well, my grandmother suddenly died and when I went to her funeral, all I could think about was how I could not shed even a single tear for her. I realized my own selfishness during that time.

I was so obsessed with myself, that I didn't take care to notice that my grandmother was suffering because of mosquitoes, cockroaches and hot weather in her house. All I could think about was how I was going to be highly educated, highly successful and rich. I was so obsessed with the 'how' and 'what' that I forgot the 'why'. And it is not that I forgot it,

I realized I never really had it from the beginning, and even if I did, it no longer resonated with me.

That death that I saw so clearly and still know so deeply every day, even now, that emptiness she left behind as she left. That's death. She was a chill-type grandmother and truth be told, I liked her even when I was very annoyed with her sometimes. She was one of a kind. And what hurts me more than anything, is the fact I still could not shed a single tear for her. Tears are markers of mourning and sadness. So, if I never shed tears, was I even sad to begin with? Now that she is gone, all I wish for is a second chance to be kinder to her. But she is gone, and I have no sure knowledge if I may meet her after my own death. That is death.

You cannot speak to others, hear others anymore or touch others anymore. You are just gone, vanished and we still have no idea what really happens to you after death. Are you in heaven or hell or erased from existence? We still don't know for sure. We only know that you will be gone, vanished and lost from this world, but you will be remembered by those who really have a connection with you. You will turn up in their minds and memories every once in a while, and disrupt all their grand plans and routines, and your memory will be with them and they will not choose to let you go, even when you are actually wasting their time and harming their productivity. They are fully aware of all that, but they still won't let you go, because you are a permanent mark in their lives and also a reminder of their own mortality.

So, this is death. A destination we all share just as we all share the journey of life, the air we breathe, the water we drink. So, beware of death and derive your 'why' considering it.

When fear of life is greater than the fear of death, suicide seems the easiest way out. But why do you fear life so much? And you have known it all your life. Death. That is the ultimate unknown. You don't know what will happen to you, to your consciousness, to your intelligence, to you at all. Meaningless life, so meaningless death. Look, people. Death will come to you. It is inevitable. Why try to rush it or delay it? It is the one single thing you're guaranteed in life. Don't be all "My life sucks and it all sucks." I have gone through it. You know what? Whatever you have, whoever you are, do something good for someone else, just out of the goodness of your heart. You can't? You can't believe in any religion for there are too many and you don't know which is the right one? Fine, just believe in goodness then. Do you follow logic? If so, then make just two assumptions about it all. By all, I mean everything and everyone. Assume that goodness is the truth, the one you can believe in whenever. Wherever it leads. Wherever it is. Assume that to be true, real, right, good, and chosen by you. Follow that path and one day you might look back on the here and now and realize "Damn, I was going about it all wrong." Why did I write this book? For the money, of course, right? No, if I wanted money, I would have written a novel instead of this book that focuses on the lost wandering souls . Just to help you and myself, because I have been there 2 times. In order to give you an idea of why, how and what to live your life for, I will share with you my priority list.

1. My Faith (Ideals)
2. All that my Faith Entails
3. My Parents
4. My True Teachers
5. Myself (My intellect and heart)
6. My Learning and such
7. My Works and such

Look, I just shared with you a very personal thing, my priority list, and I never shared that even with my parents, my friends. You, whoever you are, whatever you are, however you are, are a sharer of my intimate secrets. If you wanted a true connection in life, this is an example. I just want you to show you that there is a better path to go. You have no reason to trust or rely upon me. But if you're willing to try suicide just because you think this is the better way, why not try and test my way first? If it is fake, you can go do whatever you want. If it is right, real, true, good and chosen, then I wish you would hold on to it tightly. Do not see only what you see. See more. You may ask why to try my way. If you're cynical like me, then I know you will. It is because you think there isn't a better way or any way at all except suicide. And it's not fully your fault. Trust me on that. Your intelligence can only make sense of things you can see. It's too smart to get fooled by bogus motivational stuff. So, OK, you are a lot smarter than the average human animals out there. That's good. But that's exactly what makes you ask the big questions in life and see that lacking. There is a way other than suicide. At least test everyone out before you try something from which there is no coming back at all. All I ask for this is for just a chance for you to listen. Why am I so intent on you, a stranger? Maybe you are good or bad? I don't know, so why? Because I've gone through the same volatile mentality you are going through. I am lucky to not make that permanent mistake and genuinely afraid of that mentality but I understand it. Look, just look at the world around you . It sucks. Purely sucks. Because of Mother Nature? Yes and no. Because of mankind? Yes and no. But that doesn't mean you have to suck as well. You may not be destined for greatness, but who said anything about goodness? Trust me when I say this, goodness is also pretty rare these days. Small kindnesses are pretty rare. With what intentions should you do it? Simple, for the sake of goodness itself. And let it enter your heart from your mind and feel it. And even if you can't feel it, keep trying sincerely. And that's my message. Keep trying, sincerely, always. Who you are doesn't matter. What do you want? What are you willing to do to get it? What ideals do you uphold? Why and how and what? That is what matters. Do not seek happiness, seek contentment and progress. Do not seek death, seek purpose and goodness.

Chapter-2 (Dream)

What can I tell you about dream that you already don't know? Well, let me think.

Dreams are the same things as hopes, aspirations and the drives that actually give us a cause to act. You can say it is the projection of the outcomes your intentions and actions. Like what I dream by writing this book which is a hassle to write?

I dream a world where people will not kill themselves and even if they do, they do it to save someone else. I dream a beautiful world of selflessness and goodness. I dream a world where I won't get news that someone else killed themselves today in my country because they feared life over death or thought that death was the easiest way out. I dream that my message would spread to the farthest corners of the heart, if not by this book, by the ones who read it, by the ones who practice and preach it. I dream that we would solve the problem of suicide, by an army of Seekers instead. I dream that you , the reader, will change yourself and your life for the better after you have read this book. I dream that one day, you will be a truly successful person, will meet me and shake my hands and just say "Thank you" from the bottom of your heart so that I would realize I managed to help you. I dream that you would be better than I ever was, that you would get the honors I never got, that you would achieve the things I failed to achieve.

And after that, I also dream that I would be better for it. After all, what is the reward of goodness except goodness? Those are my dreams. They are the only reason I am writing this book, crafting my message as a gift to the world, to you. It would have been nicer if I could just give you the message myself, but I am too shy to speak to you directly, that's why I wrote a book instead, to give you, my message. Never feel indebted to me, I am nothing but dust in the vast expanse of the universe. Thank the thing that inspired me, the ideals that enriched me, the goodness that moves me. Plus, I also took some money from you for this book, so we are even. You have no debt whatsoever to me.

But you do have a debt to yourself, a duty to yourself. So use this book and my true advices for your own good. You bought it, so don't waste it. Learn from it, learn from everything and everyone. Understand it, teach it, and become a living manifestation of it. Goodness, selflessness, justice etc. are all abstract concepts. They all get manifested only through us when we adhere to them instead of our primal instincts. I want you to have a dream, a dream that truly resonates with you , even if slightly. Something that makes you feel good from the inside and something that moves you. Now if you have that dream, now carefully examine it with your mind. It may have flaws here and there, correct them. Now, embrace that dream with both your heart and mind. Let your soul embrace it, feel it and sense it.

That dream is your drive now. Keep it as your drive and let it evolve, but never vanish.

Chapter-3 (Faith)

What is 'faith'? Faith means to believe in something, anything. Faith doesn't only mean religions and their beliefs. It means any kind of belief. Believing in something greater than yourself, a higher power or a higher ideal, makes you classified as 'faithful'.

I had quite the problem with faith. After all, it cannot seen, heard or known. It's not like hope, where you can see optimism exuding from someone. Faith is more silent, more in the depths of the heart. So, I could not tell whether or not I had faith.

But as I grew , my understanding broadened and now I know what it really means. Faith is believing in something. So, if you believe in goodness, and stand up for this ideal even when the whole world is against you and your faith, you truly have faith.

In the current world, there is no shortage of hypocrites. Those who say good things just to win the recognition of the public but don't actually believe in goodness, are hypocrites. Politicians are masters at this. But let alone politicians, even children are masters at this. How do I know that?

Well, I was a hypocrite before. There are 3 reliable signs to spot a hypocrite. He who lies every time he speaks, he who doesn't keep his oaths, and he who steals others' property. Yes, I once fit the description perfectly. I'll tell you the story later.

But basically, after a certain series of events, I as a child learned the art of hypocrisy. Hypocrisy is born from deception and lies. So once you learn to lie and deceive people, you can easily become a hypocrite. I learned lying at a early age, because my parents were conservative and didn't let me do many things I wanted to do, I rather lied to them than ask for permission from them. Then, I made many promises I didn't keep, both to friends and family. Thirdly, I stole money from my own loved ones even though they would have readily given me the money had I just simply asked for it. That's how I became a hypocrite.

It's still very hard for me to stay away from hypocrisy, but I keep one simple rule for now- "to never lie again" and it works pretty well. Now, I will add my own ideas to hypocrisy. Saying that you believe in goodness and are ready to die for it and all, without actually believing in it, is outright hypocrisy, whether for show to others or to yourself.

Never lie or deceive yourself. If you do that, trust me , you will have a bad case of low self-esteem. If you do not believe in goodness, that's fine. Be honest to yourself and accept that fact, instead of deceiving yourself and others.

If you really think, know and understand that goodness is the right ideal to live with and die with, and you choose to surrender to that ideal, so that it helps you, guides you and enriches you from within , that's the right way to go. To simply surrender to that ideal is better than saying you believe in it while your heart does not have faith.

So surrender first, then hopefully, faith will enter your heart. I too didn't have any faith in any religion or goodness or anything. I purely thought this was a useless thing and a waste of my time, effort and wealth. Turns out, I was wrong. I had the intellect to learn, understand and know that truth and was luckily humble enough to accept it. So, if that is the case with you, surrender like I did to the ideal of 'goodness'. Then one day, you may achieve faith in your heart and once that faith becomes absolute, you will be the strongest you have ever been inside.

If you still cannot believe in anything, then at the very least try it out until it clicks with you. I had one more problem after choosing goodness.

What is the right religion? The right faith? The true one? There are so many religions to choose from. Religion means the way of life. There are Christianity, Al-Islam, Buddhism, Hinduism , Agnosticism, Atheism etc. religions to choose from. Which is really the right one? The absolutely correct one? If you surrender to goodness first and do right, I believe you will be guided to the right one like I was. I won't tell you the right answer.

But I will tell you that there is a right answer, and it is among the above mentioned and if you follow the instruction I gave, you will find the right answer yourself and only then, can you truly have faith. One more clue, you will find the right answer not in books, or with the tutors, but only through your own life experience. Because a sign will come to you, but unless you believe in goodness and do right and stay away from wrongdoing genuinely, you will not sense the sign. So be careful and keep your mind and heart open.

Chapter- 4 (Intentions)

Let me tell you another true story.

There was a young boy who was waiting for his mother to take him home from school. He was waiting for quite a while, but it didn't feel bad. It felt normal to him because it was a usual thing. He didn't like to play with other kids because he never saw the point in futile dangerous games where one could injure themselves easily, and thus, he didn't join his other classmates in their football game even though they invited him multiple times. Instead, he was randomly wandering on the school grounds, observing people here and there. Suddenly, his eyes fell upon his brilliant classmate, the 1st boy in his class. When we grow older, we actually respect what that means and many even get close to the brilliant students to take advantage of them. But surprisingly when we were younger, you would see that we usually boycott the most brilliant students either saying that they are nerds or that they are too arrogant to hang around with.

But this boy saw what the most brilliant student was actually feeling that time. He saw the 1st boy of his class, looking at the football game of their classmates and he saw him almost looking at them with a sense of longing. We forget that these brilliant students are still mere children however academically smart they are. They long for the normal things too like playing games with their classmates, but they tend to be a little shy and have a little pride that prevents them from asking the other classmates if they can play with them. So what do they do? They simply gaze with a sense of longing.

The young boy took pity on the 1st boy. So, he did what any innocent, naïve child would do. With his intention to be kind to the 1st boy, to be helpful, he approached the 1st boy first and asked him the question the 1st boy could not ask anyone, "Let's play a game. Will you play with me?" The 1st boy was surprised but he didn't show it and if he was happy, he didn't show that either. But he accepted and said, "Fine.

Let's play leg-kicking." The 1st boy had chosen the very game which the naïve boy hated the most. But the kind boy didn't argue and simply said, "Okay. Let's play." As for those who don't know the game 'leg-kicking', it is basically a game where children kick each other's legs with as much force they can muster to make the other one fall to the ground. You can maneuver and move as required to avoid kicks, but you cannot use hands or anything except your legs to attack.

I also don't know why people make such aggressive games. But obviously since the kind boy had the intention to help and make the other boy feel better, he didn't use his full strength for he was afraid that the other boy would get hurt.

Mind my words, most toppers in his area had thin, frail and weak bodies. Their brains eat up more nutrition from their body. So, the calculation of the kind boy was right. They started playing and both fell at the same time from each other's kicks but both of them didn't relent. Their legs stuck to each other like a knot, as they tried to make sure that the other one could not stand up, or else the one who is still laying on the ground will lose. So, the game continued as they neutralized each other's legs with their own legs, effectively creating a stalemate. As the kind boy loosened his legs' grip on the other boy to make sure the other boy didn't get hurt, the other boy instead tightened his grip. That tightened grip caused the kind boy's school pants to tear in the ass area, which revealed his underwear. The rest should be pretty obvious.

They stopped playing and the 1st boy laughed heartily at the sight , while the kind boy had no idea what to do, so he stood with his back to the wall and hid the torn place right there. He slowly went to a secluded corner of the school to hide this embarrassment. But later, a female classmate came to him there and asked if his pants really tore. The boy replied yes and pleaded with her to keep it a secret. The girl said OKAY. But the boy wanted to be extra sure, so he made her promise it. She promised right in front of him and just minutes later, came back with her friends and laughed while staring at the kind boy.

The kind boy was speechless. This was not what his parents taught him, this was not what his school taught him. They taught him the reward of goodness is goodness, not this utter embarrassment. They taught him honesty, kindness, and to keep one's promises, to help others.

Yet they didn't teach him that those who he helped may not return the same kindness they had received. That those who he helped may backstab him.

Only the 1st boy knew of the incident. The kind boy knew that fact and realized that goodness is a weakness in the real world, not a strength, nor a quality rewarded in this world, in this society of people.

So, what happened to the kind boy? Well, first he endured all that embarrassment, which , take it from me, is not easy for a little child. He waited anxiously for his mother to arrive and as soon as she did arrive, he swiftly went to her outside the school gate and only told her one part of the story- that he tore his pants while playing. Nothing else. Not the embarrassment he felt, not the realization that dawned upon him, none of that. So, what happened to the kind boy later? What did he become?

He became the worst of them. He became exclusively selfish, he didn't help others anymore and only obeyed his parents in front of them but rejected them when alone. A sense of emotionlessness swept over him. He joined the majority, successfully, and laughed with the others at anyone who tried to get out of the majority and do something good, even as little as giving someone a pen during class, when teachers want us to be strictly quiet and sit like statues.

Now that you have read the story I gave you, what is the realization you get? Ahh, it's all the kind boy's fault for being kind in the first place, or ahh, it's all the 1st boy's fault for revealing the incident in the first place.

Whatever your realization is, hold on to it. My realization is ***"In this world, good intentions do not always give birth to good outcomes for the one with the good intentions."***.

Why? I know but I won't tell you. But I want to ask you something instead. Do you have what it takes to not just have good intentions but maintain them even when the whole world may laugh at you, mock you, avoid you, torture you and even kill you? Do you have what it takes to be the kind boy in the story with the good intentions and still retain the small kind intentions even after the humiliation, or will you transform like the kind boy transformed later on?

It's easy to have good intentions but much harder to maintain them in this world. Should I tell you the name of the kind boy? His nickname is Tasin. That's right, it was me. A memory I keep to this day, and even when I am aware of it all, do you know why I transformed again into the kind, 'foolish', naïve boy?

Because when I considered all the alternatives, all the other possibilities, this one was the only one that made feel good inside, that feels something, while all others like making a load of wealth, fame , academic success, career success, etc. for myself makes me feel nothing inside. So, mock me, laugh at me, ridicule me, humiliate me and persecute me all you want, world and its people, I have found my answers, my truths and wishes. I don't have to care what you think, not anymore.

Small kindnesses are my way now, and hopefully soon, I will embody the ideals I believe in, fully , truly and absolutely, even at the cost of my academic success, my career success, my fame, my wealth and my everything.

O my readers! You can believe in goodness again, and let no one deter you from the right path again. Know that there are those who stood for the ideals you are standing for today and there are those who will be inspired by your true stories to stand for those ideals in the future. And hopefully, you will not be alone when you rise up from the sheep.

Others will be there, who are like us, and will stand for the same ideals you stand for. Even if you accidentally deviate from the right path every once in a while, come back to it. Do not leave it permanently because you feel guilty for leaving it in the first place. The ideals I believe in, includes forgiveness for those who repent and amend, with true intentions in their hearts.

And it's okay to believe in goodness because it makes you feel whole and fulfilled inside. You need at least that bit of reassurance to know you are in the right path, when the world and its people are fully against you.

So, what are your intentions? Do not get hyped up, and say "Yes, you are right! I am with you, with the same intentions you have." No, that's fanaticism, blind faith, and they can lead you to extremism and far far away from the actual goodness and faith I am teaching you here. I want you to think carefully, consider carefully and choose carefully. Make intentions you can actually stick to, genuinely. Even if it starts with small kindnesses, make sure it grows and evolves.

Chapter-5 (Actions)

Now that you have read all the previous chapters, I want to ask you how you feel? Do you feel good? Great. But if you feel nothing, then work with me a little bit longer. We are reaching the end, anyways. Try to feel your heart, even if it is dead. Try to feel the emptiness of your heart and work with that. It's a start.

Now that you have hopefully some good intentions, dreams, faith and realization of death and all, let's teach you how to design your actions, based on your intentions. Ask yourself often, if the intentions and ideals you hold in your heart, are you truly adhering to them in practice? If any course of action says no to the question and be honest about it, try your best to get out of that course of action as soon as possible. After all, you have at max 180 years to live in this world. You cannot possibly listen to all the wrong things and keep following them knowingly and when death approaches you, you repent and regret. It won't work.

You must knowingly follow the right things from the start as soon as you realize it is right. After all, death won't ask for your permission when it comes. So be aware of it much. Your actions define you, and I define you through your actions. Because I cannot see your intentions, I can only judge you based on your actions. But without the right intentions, no right action actually counts.

Let me give you an example. I personally dislike receiving coins instead of cash money . So whenever I get coins from the cashier at the shop, I simply hate carrying those slightly heavy coins in my pocket. Yes, I can be quite lazy sometimes. So, what do I do? There's always a beggar or two outside big shopping malls, so I give them the coins without much thought and without any noble intentions. But you can say, that they still received money and I still gave them charity. No, I simply disliked something and so I gave it to someone else. So, my intention is the main thing, not the action itself.

Let me give you another example to make things clearer. Let's say I have a net worth of 50 billion dollars (I actually don't, it is just an example). Now I became a bit sick, or my company is going through a tough time, so I decide to give some charity for a bit of good fortune. I randomly choose an orphanage and donate to it 1 million dollars and spread the news far and wide, declaring myself as generous and charitable.

Now another person who has a net worth of only 2 million dollars, gave away 1 million dollars to the same orphanage secretly because he actually bothered to check what the orphans themselves needed and the orphans needed more money for their healthcare bills, just 1 million dollars more. The 2nd person did the charity out of the goodness of his heart, to help the orphans even if it meant sacrificing half of his wealth.

The 2nd person could have come to me and just have asked me to donate 1 million dollars more or the orphanage regulators could have asked for more from me since they knew the orphans needed it.

But no, the charity giver gives you, the poor, even 1 dollar, and you must be thankful for their endless generosity and be polite, respectful and obedient to them. That's utterly wrong.

All of the Earth was once just a land , unowned by anyone. Just because some humans created a system of law, state , military and government doesn't mean that they are absolute.

The ancient Babylon was quite rich but look at their created systems now. Nothing but dust, lost forever in the reaches of time. But I am fine with a system that humans really tried their best to create, what I am not fine with is that many people misuse the system to fulfill their own greed. The system is our creation, and if we become corrupted, it doesn't matter how many new laws you set, or how many weapons you give to the military to enforce those laws, it is all futile. ***<u>The lack of morality is the root of all corruption in the world, always has been and always will be</u>***.

But let's go back to the example, do you think I am more generous or the 2nd person? The right question is, 'Who is truly good from among them? Whose intentions were better?" And you know the answer, it's obviously the 2nd person. He sacrificed half of his wealth to just make sure that the orphans could have enough money for their healthcare. He could have just given 50,000 dollars and people would have praised him a lot for being so generous. But he knew they needed 1 million dollars and so he gave them the full amount they needed, not a single dollar less. I, on the other hand, would be thinking 'Why hasn't my good fortune come yet?'.

That's the difference between true goodness and apparent goodness. I am also a work in progress, but I showed you the direction that I want to go towards, the destination I wish to reach and the aim I strive for. Whatever you truly strive for, get your actions in line with them.

You may ask, 'What should be my intention for doing good works and such?'. Well, my answer is 'For the sake of goodness itself'. It means that you stand for an ideal, not just for a single person, but an ideal that lived before you, lives on in you and will live on after you as well. Why do you think so many people fought wars and sacrificed themselves? Because they lived, fought and died for an ideal, an ideal they deeply believed in. So much so that that ideal shone into existence through them, and was immortalized by the writers who saw it and wrote them down.

What actions can you take? If you want specific instructions from me, then I will tell you. If not, I won't bother wasting my time nor yours. But for those who need a bit of instructions, I will give you that:

1. Wake early at 5:00 am everyday by sleeping at 9:00 pm every night, even during holidays. Obviously, there may be times when you have something more important, then it is fine to modify this rule. But make sure you get enough rest. Enough rest ensures that your mind has clarity and you can function in life properly. (Plus, most cases of depression ,anxiety and such comes from an unhealthy sleep routine. So be careful.)

2. Eat fruits as much as possible. They are not tasteless like vegetables are and are pretty nutritious.

3. Remember, all of the world and its people are under you in your mind. They cannot take precedence before you yourself in your case. So, keep things like curriculars, co-curriculars, and such under you in your case. They do not rule over you, nor should you let them. They are under you , because it is your choice whether or not to give them time and effort. And have time every day for yourself at least 30 minutes, for anything you want to do, whether to think about life , your decisions and all , or to simply look at nature. This is your life, your time and your potential. You can choose how to use it. Don't let exams nullify this 'me' time.

4. You can ignore school, college and university and all of that formal stuff. But do not ignore knowledge. Learn from everything and everyone, but only choose what is good and useful from among them to enrich you. I personally read a lot of books and through them, I get a sense of how vast and deep knowledge really is. I even read books of the formal curriculum because even they have something to teach me. Books are my best teachers. Because I am usually a bit slow to understand,

they let me take as much time as I need to understand them. They are not my friends, but they are my teachers.

5. Exercise for 15 minutes every morning after you wake up. (if you want, I could tell you my personal exercise routine, but I would like to keep it private)

6. Finally, do only a 5 minute to 10-minute meditation every night before going to bed.

Just hold on to the above 6 steps and I can promise you, you are taking a step towards progress. You don't have to be perfect, because you can never be perfect. Not even I am perfect, and I am obsessed with utter perfection. Life should not be a pursuit for perfection, it should only be a pursuit of progress, real and genuine.

Chapter- 6 (Resilience)

Now, if you have read this far serially, I congratulate you. You have the tiniest bit of resilience. Why so less? Well, because this book is not even a 100 paged book. And not to brag , but I have read 500 paged books.

So yeah, the resilience needed here was quite low. But thankfully, you have that tiny bit, which means you have something you can grow and evolve. That's why I am here.

You may have loved the book, liked it, or disliked it or hated it or felt nothing at all. But if you hated it and still read this far sequentially, I must applaud your resilience. In this world where new changes are constantly happening and good people are constantly hit with newer and harder struggles when they are following the right path, you must be resilient. If you sway every time someone rebukes you, beats you, or threatens you, you lack resilience within you.

The only way I know so far to cultivate resilience is to have a specified strong intention in your heart and which you can remember easily with your mind every time you feel like you need it. Additionally, you need quite the confidence in yourself . And the only way to achieve that is to be always honest to yourself, keep your promises to yourself, and never harm yourself. You may have noticed that these represent the 3 signs of a hypocrite. Basically, in order to have self-confidence, you must never be a hypocrite at least to yourself. Sounds easy enough, but it may be hard for some. So be careful and be aware of it.

Let me tell you a final true story before I end this book. In my childhood, I was quite stubborn. If I wanted something, I went out and got it, where it was academic awards or toys or even other things. But the thing is, after I got it, all my routine and discipline I had before, vanished. Discipline and resilience are two things I would like to have at all times and at all cases.

But the truth is, we cannot always be resilient and disciplined. There will be times when we are vulnerable, and that is exactly the time when you must hold on to discipline no matter what. If you can do that, I can say to you with certainty that you can achieve almost anything. People like to think there is only one secret to success. But truth be told, there are more than one key to success. The keys include first the 'why' (the reason that drives you no matter what happens) , the 'how' (the process you choose to achieve success), the 'what' (the outcomes you envision). All of them require purpose, consistency, discipline, small adjustments in the approach and faith to create and maintain. The final true story is this:

I was utterly lost 2 times in my life inside myself. The first time was during the Covid pandemic and the 2nd time was quite recently. Since my mind can consider so many different ideas, thoughts and possibilities all at once, it made me utterly confused and utterly lost. As I said before, I read a lot of books, and each book is about an idea that expands into sub ideas and such. Whenever I got multiple points of view on the same topic, it confused me and I didn't know what to trust anymore. As such, all of my systems created out of previously read books fell down miserably and while I knew that I can revive them anytime, I stalled and thought instead, whether it would be right or wrong to revive them . That stalling becomes a year or two somehow. And by the end, I am usually so lost that I lose everything. The only way to make sure that never happens is the 2nd assumption. Assume that everything you know except the 1st assumption is testable, changeable and therefore improvable.

With that, the 2nd assumption is basically, ***"Everything you know except the 1st assumption is testable, changeable and therefore improvable"*** . If you think that your life sucks, that you're just a burden , that death is the easiest way out, I ask you to test that knowledge against real-life, in such a way you can correct your knowledge afterwards and change for the better. That's exactly what I do.

In my toughest times, I wrote a diary. Do you know what is the single statement repeated over and over in that diary? ***<u>"I will not give up on myself no matter what, in this world."</u>***

Never give up on yourself, especially during your worst times because if I had given up then, I could have never proved to myself that I was still capable of academic success, career success and most importantly, inner success. I will give you my 3 laws of that success as my parting gift to you, the 3 laws I held on to every day during that critical time of my life when I felt like giving up, felt like my world was crumbling around me, felt that death was the easiest way out, when I even sincerely prayed for death. Luckily, the wish didn't come true then but will come true soon. Before I die, before my voice is silenced by death, before my time ends and before I go away, I shall share with you the 3 laws that gave me success, if used truly to their core, may give you too the success you so deeply need and want.

1<u>st</u> Law: *"**More than enough thinking has been done.**"* (These days, we tend to overthink, so just stop your conscious chains of thinking. Let the thinking happen naturally instead, and if it disturbs you, stop thinking. You need to stop thinking, when you know that it is going to prove harmful instead. And yes, thinking can be harmful.)

2<u>nd</u> Law: *"**I have no time nor capacity for doubts, hesitations, fears or distractions. So, no doubts, hesitations, fears or distractions, ever.**"* (You really have no time for doubts, fear, hesitations or distractions, you do not know when death may come upon you. It may be right here right now as you are reading this line, so it is better to assume you have no time and nor any capacity for such. Because, whenever you are doing something you know you should do, you don't have any capacity for doubts, hesitations, fears or distractions.)

<u>3rd Law:</u> *"As long as I can still work on it, I must work on it always no matter what."* (If you can still work on yourself , your life, your career, your family, your contribution to all, your moral character, your intentions, your interests, your education and anything, then you must work on it. And truth be told, as long as you are alive, you can still work on any or even all of them. If you need advice on how, you can contact me at my email address.)

Additional Chapter (The Mass Uprising of 2024)

I really didn't want to add this chapter. Why? Because it could put me in real mortal danger and also because of the hassle to write another few pages. But here it goes, for I must strive to live for the ideals I teach. And truth be told, only my pen name is in this book, so I should be fine or at least, I hope. I still , after all, have some work and duty left to fulfill first before I die.

Let me tell you another true story. And don't worry, this time, it may be better than all those before.

Once upon a time, some good, educated young people realized the system was being unfair to them and the public. They didn't have any high-level connections and came from humble families, nor were they affiliated with any political party, let alone the ruling party's branch party 'The Students' League'.

So, they did what anyone would, for the sake of fairness, they first submitted a case to their national court. But the case was not given any importance at all, let alone addressed properly.

The young people realized what every grown-up in the country already knew – that their justice system was a big failure. Why? Because they took money, vast amounts of money as court charges, but the cases sat there in the courts for year after year.

In fact, there is even a joke in the country, that if you want to annoy someone or irritate someone, let's say your 'mortal enemy'. And let's say that you two live in the same city in the very north of the country as well.

All you had to do was simply file a case (it can be a false or nonsense case, no problem) against him at a court in a city or town 1,000 kilometers away from your enemy's city directly in the south.

Your enemy would then have to travel all the way to that court in that city 1,000 kilometers away, with his own transport fees and will be forced to postpone all his important activities and business deals he may have.

Not just that, if he doesn't comply and go to the court 1, 000 kilometers away from his home every time he is summoned, he will be arrested and will have to pay bail to get free. It's the perfect revenge, where you can tire your enemy financially, physically and mentally.

After all, the court process is unnecessarily burdensome, exhausting and even futile in the end.

Let me give another real-life example. A very experienced doctor with great skills, with great academic records and a large number of patients who seek his service, goes to court to file a case against his senior doctors, the professors, in his hospital.

Why the case? Because he is not being promoted from consultant to Assistant Professor in rank, even though, by his age and expertise, he should have been a fully-fledged Professor by now.

In fact, his promotion is being delayed and constantly postponed year after year. And now, it has been over 10 years. Still nothing happened. I have met the man myself, a very generous and generic religious guy who donates to charity secretly for the good of his soul and because he genuinely feels pity for the poor people, the orphans and the poor relatives. He is my personal doctor and he constantly rebukes me whenever I do something that's medically not allowed for me.

Yet, even though his intentions are good and he does good, what happens? His promotion, something he should have received a decade ago, an honor and a prestige is being denied to him repeatedly. And it's not like the poor man didn't try other means.

He prayed to his God in his religion, he did good, he was good to his parents and his family. Heck, he even gave a series of large sums of money as bribes to get his due. Because he is desperate, his juniors, are getting promoted to Professor ranks and they mock him, they ridicule him and they humiliate him, even though he is the senior, with the more expertise and patients.

This man went against this injustice in every way he could. He filed a case in court and even won the case and the court told the authorities to give him his proper rank.

But the authorities still don't do anything, except delaying and delaying again that promise and keep taking large bribes from the good doctor without ever fulfilling their end of bargain. Even though the court gave its final verdict after 10 long years , during which time, the court obviously took large amounts of money from the good doctor, the hospital authorities themselves still roam free and no police ever comes for them even though they refused to follow a direct court order and obviously the court itself doesn't do anything more.

If you want to complain against them for refusing to follow the court order and delaying that long-due promotion, welcome to the court again and please pay the court charges and wait another 10 years for another futile court order.

You may ask, well what did the good doctor do to deserve this hellish punishment? I'll tell you what he did, he was a medical student at a medical university decades ago and he supported an opposition party instead of the current ruling party. That's literally all he did wrong.

The bribes weren't wrong, no, they are called 'speed money' in this country , to speed up the process of the government authorities. Like hell bribes weren't wrong. Of course they are wrong!

And I chastised the good doctor for it. I said, "Don't mix goodness with evil, don't mix rightness with wrongness." But of course, the good doctor didn't listen, he was so helpless that he had no other way. He desperately wanted his promotion and now he stays put and doesn't bark anymore, doesn't bite anymore. Why?

Well, he tried a lot of ways, and he now knows it is all futile. So, he simply surrenders to the injustice and unfairness and bears with it. I am simply thankful that he didn't kill himself, for his religion promises judgement after death, true justice after death. Too bad his religion doesn't promise it before death.

I just gave you 2 real-life examples of the justice system in practice. In the books and documents, the justice system is near-perfect, all good.

But in actual practice, the system is a big failure, not because the system itself is bad, but because the people who run it are corrupt.

Let's say we turn the situation around and make the party that the good doctor supported so long ago, the ruling party. You will see the same injustice happening to the supporters and members of the opposition party. Why, how and what?

Yes, because people can get corrupt when in power, because they think they are untouchable and that is the reality outside of the books that they teach you at your educational institutions, at least in this country.

Let me tell you another fun fact, in order to get proper jobs and promotions at those jobs in this country, you have to be either a family member or pay large bribes to the seniors at that institution (whether government or private sectors) or have to be an exceptional genius, someone they can easily take advantage of.

Let's go back to the main story, to the good young people. Faced with no other effective alternative, they missed their attendances in their universities and instead, they organized movements and protests throughout their country to fight against injustice because the justice system miserably failed to give them justice.

Initially, all of the movements were peaceful and without any violence. They blocked major main roads and politely asked each uncle and aunty to please take rickshaws instead of their cars or to walk. And the uncles and aunties may have felt a bit annoyed but they still admired the efforts of these young people which reminded them of their own university movements in their university days. So, the protests and movements continued.

The government felt that they were being a nuisance, you know, like some ants walking around on your foot. So they did what they thought , should be done, to mere nuisances. They squashed them literally. How?

Well, they sent both the police and the Students' League (a branch of the ruling party itself, where these students who enjoyed the extra benefits of large sums of money to buy expensive motorcycles and whatnot, obeyed directly the government's orders , for they too are the government lackeys. It was their duty to keep all the students, whether any student was of any political party or not, in line to enjoy their privileges. I'll expand on them later, but they are basically the bad students, not the good ones who are protesting right now) .

Both the police and the Students' League had live bullets and live guns. So, they shot at the students directly and killed some of them and injured most others.

Now that they thought that they had done their duty, they went back to their carefree life of taking bribes from auto-rickshaw pullers, bus drivers and so on. Auto-rickshaw is a kind of rickshaw (light and small vehicle, you can look it up on Google) which is not legally allowed in the country because the government claims that the technology is unstable and can cause accidents.

To that opinion, I call flagrant deception and lack of responsibility. Look, they are poor people who don't want to pull the normal rickshaws physically anymore, like their fathers and grandfathers did. Someone installed a technology on the rickshaw so that they don't have to pull anymore, and can move more easily and faster.

But instead of perfecting the technology and teaching these poor uneducated people how to properly use them, the government banned it altogether and now the auto-rickshaw pullers must pay 1 dollar worth of money every day to the police and the members of the students League in the area they operate at.

They only earn a few dollars worth of money each day if they are really lucky, and you want them to bribe the police everyday whether or not they even earned any money?

Let's give it a clap, let's give a cheer for the just government, whose duty it is to safeguard and enrich every citizen of the country, even the poor people, especially them. What's the point of democracy if the power is only held by the powerful and the powerful are obedient first and foremost to the super-rich who paid for the election campaigns and all?

Anyways, back to the main story, the government felt satisfied after ordering the police to shoot live bullets at the students because the movements stopped for the moment.

Let me tell what they were most likely thinking. They thought that by shooting and killing some students and injuring others, they had successfully instilled fear in the students.

They thought that the students , out of fear of their own lives and best interests, would give up the protest and obediently follow the government's instructions (which are actually orders).

But no, the young students, who dream of justice and fairness in an unjust and cruel world, didn't relent. Instead, they restarted protests and movements with a new vigor and a new purpose.

"For the sake of goodness, for the sake of fairness and justice." They rose up with higher numbers and even greater determination. I must say, such courage and bravery deserve some praise. Even I admire them, even though I can be quite cynical at times.

But when you put your own life and your own best interests at risk , even willing sacrifice them for an ideal you believe in or for someone else, I must say my heart melts at the sight, so much so that I would trust you more than anyone else.

It is the stories we read, saw on television, and grew up admiring in our childhoods, the fiction becoming reality, the miracle becoming the norm and the heart becoming inspired.

The government thought, "Oh shit. Their numbers have increased. Fine, let us then release the entirety of the Police, our Student Parties(the bad students) ,the Brutal Action Force and even the Border Guard on them. What can they possibly do against live guns, sound grenades and tear gas?"

Let me remind you that the good guys are simply students, young, brave and with a dream, a purpose. They are from the top universities in the country, students who got scholarships and are academically gifted and talented. They are the future of any nation, the future engineers, the future doctors, the future businessmen etc. Basically, what I am trying to say, is that they are smart.

So, what do you do against armed and trained forces who have real guns and advanced weapons all in their disposal, paid for the taxes you yourself have given everyday since you were born? What can you possibly do? And you have no gun, because civilians cannot have guns per the country law. And you have no money, no funds and nothing to actually fight against them properly. They can shoot a single bullet in your brain and suddenly you are dead and all of your thoughts, academic achievements(both current and future), your career etc. are all null and void.

Well, a clash was inevitable at this point as students took up protests and movements all across the country especially at the capital.

The entirety of the Police, the Action forces, and the Border Guard comes for you all students no matter your great numbers. They shoot at you with rubber bullets and sometimes even live ones. They release tear gas and sound grenades, all to disrupt you, to make you submit. Suddenly, they again shoot live bullets which hits the head of some of your closest true friends, with whom you laughed and joked just weeks ago and with whom you had plans to visit the beach in the next winter.

And your heart feels fear, and your mind wants to run away and yet you stay where you are. And still, you rise up and you fight with a wooden stick in your hand against the onslaught of the armed forces and a rubber bullet hits your right leg and you fall on the hard ,rough road , and then a live bullet hits your hand and you feel the unbearable pain and still you try to move, try to stand up. Finally, they shoot a live bullet to your head. And you simply die away, knowing your purpose was the right one.

That's what happened with hundreds of students during that time. As the British say, 'It was a bloody mess, literally'. They all were injured at the very least, whether physically or emotionally or psychologically. And many of them saw their friends die, saw even innocent civilians die who were just passing through. Dead bodies of shot students and civilians lay at the streets and also at the staircases of some buildings where the students tried to hide themselves from the gunfire. A truly grim picture it was, for anyone who saw it. So much so that anger awakens in your heart, and pure hatred for the corrupt authorities and their ever-obedient lackeys.

The good students still didn't relent. Truth be told, if I was in their place, I would have relented by then. But the good students had another idea instead.

They were angry now and filled with vengeance in their hearts. So, if you release fire at us, we will return it. That's how they retaliated, fire with fire. They bought petrol from the petrol pumps with what little money they had , and used that petrol to burn the police boxes, to burn the government officials' expensive cars (which they bought with the taxes paid by us) , to burn government structures and with the help and support of the general public, beat the hell out of some corrupt ministers and even their bodyguards.

I'll admit it was a wrong move, to burn down government stuff like that. Not because I support the corrupt government. Quite the opposite, it is because the reality is that, if all the clashes end finally , the government will again approve a big budget and rebuild those structures with taxes paid by us.

Not just that, the government officials will most assuredly, sneakily take away a big portion of the budget money into their own pockets. I am actually surprised the corrupt government officials themselves don't burn their own government buildings and structures. The profits would be enormous for them.

There is a very credible idea that the ruling party members themselves set fire to some of their own government buildings so that they could show the international community, the ambassadors residing in the country, that it was the good students who damaged them and employed violence first and as a major side benefit, they would get the profits later when they rebuild it all with tax money. With that, the international community would not know what to believe and stand still. That's their tactic and it actually works.

I must commend the corrupt government officials for their cunningness. The right move by the good students would have been to burn the corrupt government officials themselves and their own private houses and cars.

It may seem extreme, but it is not extreme but perfectly just and right since it was the corrupt government officials who ordered the shooting of the good students in the first place.

So what happened after the fires were set? Well, the government imposed a nationwide ban on all movements except its own party's and imposed Section-144, basically no movements can be done by the students or they will be killed or arrested or tortured.

Even so, the good students still didn't relent. I must commend them for their resilience. They again took to the streets with new demands of justice for their killed classmates, seniors and juniors.

And this time, they had the public support , even some people giving free food and shelter to them. Why?

Because all the good students were no longer safe in their university hostels. Because the Students' League, the bad students, harassed and even attacks them there regularly and even the police entered the university grounds to attack the good students now.

So, the situation got worse and worse. The government now became afraid of the good students. So, they immediately summoned the military forces and turned off the internet for a whole week.

Now, you may think 'Why turn off the internet precisely the time you summon the military forces?'.

Because if the internet was on, the students could warn each other and coordinate better and so that the grim pictures of students shot and killed, of their dead head-shot bodies lying side by side each other in their own hostel room, are not spread on social media.

Because then the public will rise, and international community will rise against the current government. So, they turned off the internet for a whole week and only God knows best how many they secretly killed during that time.

The official records say only 163 people were killed by the corrupt authorities. But I know more were killed. How? Man, of course I would notice if many of my acquaintances suddenly vanish into thin air. Of course, I would notice the helicopter always making rounds above my own hotel, and of course I would hear and see the live bullets being shot at the good students and civilians from the helicopter and of course my eyes will see the dead body of a mere 6 year-old child, who was simply playing football on the road with his father just moments ago.

Of course, I would feel a sudden numbness when I see the father holding his dead child with tears in his dark-brown eyes. Of course, I would feel even despair when I see a young man's face slashed bloodily by a bullet wound and his dark-red blood flowing from a small hole in his black-haired head.

I'll tell you the real order that the government gave to the military forces, without changing a single word. The order was *"Shoot to kill"* and thankfully some of the good students became aware of the order from their teacher whose brother was in the army but they couldn't spread the message fast enough because the internet was shut down just minutes later.

I know how unreliable news and information can be. In fact, if you opened any TV channel under the government, (which is most of the channels), you will see the situation is normal, that some innocent police were attacked by the violent cruel protesters, that the police are doing everything in their power to protect all citizens of the country.

Such blatant lying and such blatant hypocrisy. You know how I judge news or information to be true? I look at it from all sides, especially the opposite side and only believe from the reliable sources (which is usually few and really hard to find).

Let me tell you what drives these good students, the unrelenting protesters. Their beautiful ideals, morality and faith drive them. They are normal students from the top universities in the country.

They are not stupid. But people will call them 'foolish'. Why? Because these good students should have just remained obedient to the government, to the government's lackeys i.e. the Students' League leaders and members, Police etc.

If they did so, they could have easily gone through university and get a high-paying job and marry and have children and our society would have respected them a lot.

But inside, they would lose their goodness, their integrity and they knew that if they simply submitted to how the world was, they could never see what the world could be. Let me tell you a bit about the students.

These students hail from humble families. Their fathers are rickshaw pullers, small businessmen and such. They hail from the villages. But they are academically smarter than the city students and more purer inside.

But when they enter university in the cities, they become victims of a political hierarchy inside the university. Plus, since they hail from villages, they have to stay in hostels with the bullies themselves. The leaders and members of the Students' League force these good students out of their rooms , disrupting their studies and making them do their chores.

The better the student is, academically, the more they pester and disturb him. Moreover, they forcefully grab the allowances the good students get from their hard-working poor parents from the rural areas.

Basically, education alone is immense mental torture and you add this unbearable, unjust and unfair torture to the mix, the good students cannot bear it anymore.

There is a quota system in all the public universities of the country. Basically, the children, grandchildren and relatives of the freedom fighters who fought in the Liberation War of country over 5 decades ago, keep almost 30% of the available seats in the public universities.

As a result, even if the child of a random rickshaw puller has more merit , marks and talent than the grandchild of a rich relative of a freedom fighter , the latter would get accepted into the public university. And getting accepted to the public university is like getting a fully funded scholarship for the students of this country.

So, it should be obvious who needs it more and who is worthy more of getting that scholarship. That's why, when the good students realized the quota system is indeed unfair. All of their frustrations aimed at fixing that simple injustice first.

They themselves didn't need to care whether their juniors got justice or not. But the thing is , they did care and they sacrificed their lives to ease the burden of the juniors who may not even know or remember them.

With the military forces in action, the situation has been forcefully fixed by the government now. But tensions remain high, and sources confirmed at least 1000 people were killed, 10,000 students arrested , and their leaders in police custody, where God knows how much torture they must be enduring, if not already dead.

The government is not all bad. They accepted the quota reform demand at least in appearance and reviewed the ruling in it and changed it from 70% to 91.6% seats available for the public, all in just 2 days.

Remember when I told you, that the country's court rulings take years and years for everyone. Turns out, it is not for everyone because the government can effectively overrule the court and increase its ruling speed a hundred times more on command.

Plus, the lawyer representing the government in the court must be the best lawyer in the world. How the hell did he convince the judge to approve the new quota system in just 2 days, when it should normally take weeks, if not months?

Seems like the government controls the justice system, not the other way around. When this ruling was happening, 3 student leaders of the good students came forth to review it. After reviewing the document, they realized that the new law had a tiny problem. The government sneaked in a little clause in it that allows them to change it back whenever they want.

Like I said, these good students are smart and so they went to the media and spoke out against the government. They also had other demands, including justice for the slaughtered good students, and the stepping down of the illegal government. They also stated that they were afraid that the authorities' lackeys will pick them up from the streets as soon as the media goes away.

And they were right. Because the detective branch of police dutifully captured them and put them in custody and stated to the media it was for the good student leaders' own safety. I sometimes think, do they really think we are that stupid? Ahh, what a world we live in.

You may be interested to know why the good students accused the government to be illegal. Well, let me take you to the past, 15 years earlier, when the current party was elected through democratic elections.

After being elected however, they showed their true colors and forgot the people who elected them in the first place.

They soon became dictators and the public obviously didn't like them anymore. So, obviously they would lose the next elections .

The ruling party members realized that and so, they rigged up the next elections. So when you would go to vote, they would say to you, "You have already voted." and you would be surprised and ask, "Really, who did I vote for? I forgot completely." And they would recognize the sarcasm in your voice and swiftly call the police to escort you out.

In fact, there was a funny incident as well. A voter can only vote in his birth region. Let's say there were 500,000 voters in a region, so logically, only 500,000 was the maximum number of votes a party could have from that region, but after the polls, it was found that the party had received 650,000 votes from that region.

Wow, what a miracle! No, not really, the current ruling party didn't even bother to steal the votes properly. And obviously the local public knew what really happened and even the international community knew what really happened. What did they do?

They simply negatively commented on it and did nothing else. So, obviously the current ruling party became more and more out of control. Because Albert Einstein, a well-known physicist, said it best and I quote him, "The world will not destroyed by those who do evil, but by those who watch them without doing anything."

It is our fault that we are like this. So, it's time to take responsibility for our actions and the actions of others.

Let's go back to the main story. The students are now still fighting and God knows best what is in store for them and the country people. Another catastrophe or a miracle? They don't know and yet they hope for the latter. They are still fighting and if they die, next it must be us who must fight and after us, others will take our place.

Can you guess the country I am talking about? Fortunately or unfortunately, the longest sea beach in the world is in that country and I just had to go there to check it out exactly at the time the good students decided to rise up.

I can't complain really, because I am witnessing firsthand a revolution in the making- the Mass Uprising of 2024.

I would not have previously written their story if I was not in the country during the time. Why? Because I wouldn't have cared much. Why should you and me care about what happens in a foreign country? For the sake of goodness, which includes empathy. For it could happen to you and me any day that a mad, brutal dictator who managed to win the elections and then showed their true colors and took over the whole country forever, and executed anyone who questioned their authority.

How can we make a difference? Either by fighting against it, or speaking out against it or supporting the country people themselves however we can. What would that do? It will make an impact, and will prove that the international community are not just a bunch of hypocrites, who only will comment against the government and do nothing else.

By the way, the country is Bangladesh, a small country in South Asia and the mad-cruel dictator is a true master in the art of hypocrisy, surpassing even my previously hypocritic self. Who is the person? Why don't you see for yourself? A simple search on Google should help.

The story I have talked about may seem specific to a country with a specific corrupt authority, but this is actually, at its core, a universal story. The same core pattern has repeated in the past, is repeating in the present and will most likely repeat in the future as well.

Which side of the story do you genuinely, from the bottom of your heart, want to be in? Do you want be the heroic, selfless and brave good students?

Or do you want to be the corrupt authorities? Or do you want to be the scared and complacent public? Or those few in the public who help the good students however they can? Or do you want to be the ineffective and hypocritical international community?

It is your choice. You must make the choice as I made mine. If you are truly the reader I dedicated my book towards, you should know, feel and understand the choice I made. The moment I decided to add this chapter, it was the moment I had made my choice.

Do you know what happens to people here who speak out against the government? Of course, you do. And now that I have done exactly that, what do you think the choice I made was?

To be the 'foolish', naïve and kind boy yet again, with one key difference, to be that boy forevermore no matter what anyone says, does and thinks. This is my choice, a choice I am willing to live for , fight for and finally even die for. Why? "For the sake of goodness."

What's your choice and your intention ?

.

My Ending Note to the Reader

First of all, congratulations. You managed to finish a book that took me over 3 weeks to finish and I had to call upon all my decades of life experience to write it.

I can only hope that you have read and understood the book properly and if I managed to convince you that your life deserves another shot, that you deserve another shot, your future in the world deserves another shot, that goodness deserves another shot, it is enough for me.

When I wrote this book, I was worried that I was not really the person who deserved to extend my hand to you, to help you and to enrich you within. But thankfully, I can say that like you too who is struggling through life, I am also struggling through life and we both can strive to do our best. And when we'll meet, we can compete on goodness, instead of at education, career, wealth etc. So please, prepare yourself for that day, as I will too prepare myself for being better inside, as each year of life slips by.

If you need any advice or help regarding anything , I can direct you to some pretty reliable sources and if you want, I can also give you my personal advice, which I'll admit, I was stingy with before.

Yeah, I used to think every knowledge shared meant both the competition and me got better which basically translates to the fact that we stayed equal to each other after gaining that knowledge. But we all want to be better than the others, and that's fine.

Be better than all others in goodness. I too will try my best and all I can ask from you, is to do your best and trust the Truth whatever it is.

Thank you greatly for your time, for your efforts and for giving yourself another chance. I give you the good news of inner success and the warning of a painful situation should you choose to abandon the right path knowingly.

As for the sign indicated before, time to reveal it.

The sign's first upper part at the very start I showed actually indicated all the various, different and unique possibilities of everything, everyone and all. And the second part of the sign, just below it at the right, indicated the possibilities within a single possibility and it goes on and on. When you think like that, everything else just simply pales in comparison. It's like internalizing the very concept of infinity upon infinity itself. So vast and so deep that all else is just nothing compared to it.

Just like the sky, just like the oceans, and just like the stars above. If you ever feel too bad, just take refuge in nature. It is neither selfish like humans nor limited in size. If you cannot see anything else, just look at the sky, how vast and how majestic it really is. All your worries just pale away when you really realize it all. Anyways, goodbye and do your best. Whatever you are struggling with, it is within your capacity to overcome it. How do I know that? Like I said, I know some things with absoluteness. So, trust that sense and do your best.

With the ideals that bind us forever,
Tasin SCiva.

30th July 2024

A Poem By Tasin SCiva

The Seekers of Truth

"Those who seek
Are no longer meek.
Those who seek
Are no longer weak.
'But what to seek, how and why? '
There is such a cry.
To them, I say
To seek the Truth Ray.
To them, I say
By letting go, in the 'goodness' bay
To them, I say
Because it is the Right Way.
So let us be united
No longer divided.
So let us be good
No longer rude.
So let us be right
No longer a blight.
So let us be the Seekers
No longer deceptive speakers."

About the Author

Tasin SCiva is the pen name of the author. Due to the nature of his book content, he wishes to keep his identity a secret. But you can contact him at his email address- tasinsciva346@gmail.com, only if you have any further questions or need. He also has a X (formerly Twitter) account @TasinSCiva45 .

He is also a human being, a wanderer and a seeker. He reads a lot of books and likes spending time with nature. He is mainly a writer of fiction, but wanted to leave behind a book for suicidal people like him.

He likes to read books, both fiction and non-fiction. He also likes to be fit and travels around a lot whenever possible. He is so open to new ideas that he sometimes gets insane from them. But insanity is only chaos in the mind and by understanding that, he recreates order peacefully inside his mind.

He's honest, sometimes brutally honest and sometimes politely honest. And while he struggles to always maintain the right intentions in his heart, he does his best whenever possible. His only wish is for the reader to give life, goodness and selflessness another shot. He tend to be late at events and his only reply to that is *"Better late than never"*.